KENYA

KENYA

Zachery Winslow

CHELSEA HOUSE

LV13-003087

Library of Congress Cataloging-in-Publication Data

Winslow, Zachery.
   Kenya.
   Includes index.
   Summary: Surveys the history, topography, people, and culture of Kenya,
with an emphasis on its current economy, industry, and place in the
political world.

   1. Kenya. [1. Kenya]
   I. Title
   DT433.522.G47   1987   967.6'2   86-33411

   ISBN 1-55546-169-7

Project Editor: Elizabeth L. Mauro
Associate Editors: Rafaela Ellis, Laurie Goodman
Chief Copy Editor: Melissa Padovani
Art Director: Maureen McCafferty
Series Designer: Anita Noble
Project Coordinator: Kathleen P. Luczak
Production Manager: Brian A. Shulik

Contents

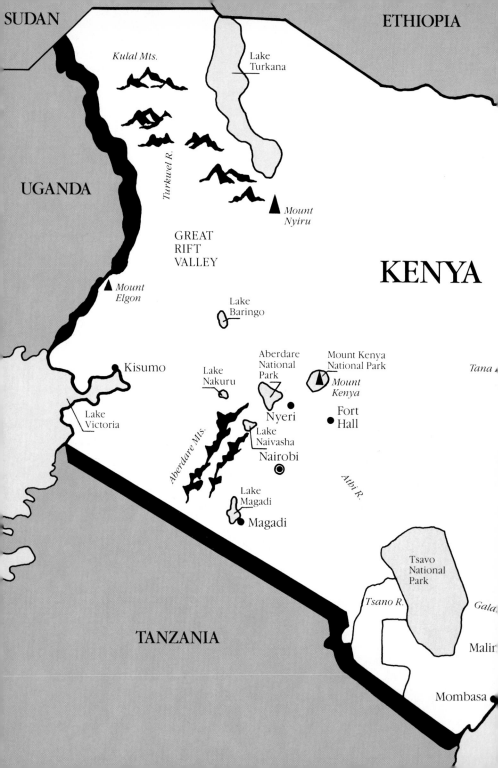

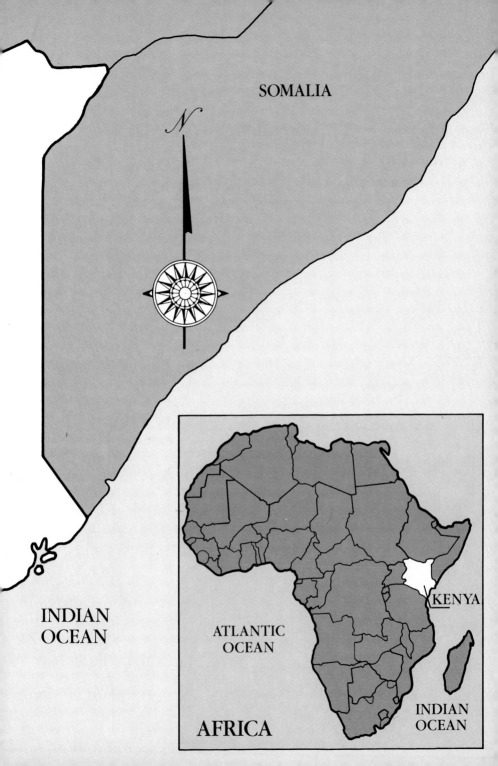

SOMALIA

N

INDIAN
OCEAN

ATLANTIC
OCEAN

KENYA

AFRICA

INDIAN
OCEAN

An Ancient New Republic

Ever since the protohuman species *homo habilis* settled there in 2 million B.C., people have flocked to the lush and fertile land known today as Kenya. Its natural seaports, miles of shoreline, and productive soil have lured Arabs, Portuguese, Britons, and dozens of African ethnic groups to Kenya.

Historians can trace the origins of modern Kenya to 400 B.C., when people began migrating there from other parts of the continent. In the 8th century A.D., Arab traders came to Kenya from North Africa and the Arabian peninsula. In the 15th century, Portuguese sailors landed on the East African coast and began the first of many struggles by foreign powers to control Kenya. Soon, other European countries became interested in farming Africa's fertile soil, and by the late 19th century Great Britain was acquiring land in Kenya.

By 1905, most of East Africa was under British rule. Although the British brought many improvements to Kenya (most notably modern medicine and education), they also repressed and exploited the native population. In the 1920s, native Kenyans began to organize, and for the next 40 years they demanded—often through violence—a voice in their government. In 1963, Kenya's native peo-

Kenya was under British rule for more than 60 years before it became an independent nation in 1963

ple finally forced the British to surrender control of the country, and the era of colonial domination ended.

Since gaining independence, Kenya has become the political and economic leader of East Africa. Its diverse peoples are learning to live together and to utilize the best features of their many cultures to build a strong Kenya.

9

Looming Mountains and Fertile Valleys

The Republic of Kenya covers an area of 224,960 square miles (582,650 square kilometers) on Africa's eastern coast. It borders the Indian Ocean to the southeast and shares boundaries with five other African nations—Tanzania, Uganda, Sudan, Ethiopia, and Somalia. Together, Kenya, Tanzania, and Uganda are known as East Africa.

The beauty and diversity of Kenya's landscape have attracted visitors for thousands of years. The varied terrain includes arid plains, lush grasslands, looming mountains, and fertile valleys. The country is cut in two by the Great Rift Valley, which runs from Lake Turkana in the northwest to Lake Natron on the Tanzanian border. The valley is between 30 and 40 miles (48 and 64 kilometers) wide and between 2,000 and 3,000 feet (610 and 915 meters) deep, and it is one of the most striking features of Kenya's landscape. At its center, near Lake Naivasha, the rift is between 6,000 and 7,000 feet (1,850 and 2,150 m) above sea level. From this high point, it descends in a series of step-like formations, reaching its lowest elevations at its northern and southern extremes.

Kenya consists of four major geographical regions: the southeast coastal plains, the northeast thornbush plains, the northwest

Kenya's southwest highlands plateau, the country's most fertile region, provides excellent grazing for cattle

scrubland, and the southwest highlands. Except for the mountains of the Teita Hills range, which rise to about 7,000 feet (2,150 meters), the southeast coastal plains are almost totally flat. Because the region suffers from insufficient rainfall, most coastal residents live in the irrigated areas around the port city of Mombasa or in the valley surrounding the Tana River.

In the dry thornbush plains of the northeast coastal and inland regions, yearly rainfall is less than 20 inches (500 millimeters). This area is barren and inhospitable, and few Kenyans live here. Its chief inhabitant is the dreaded tsetse fly, carrier of sleeping sickness, a serious tropical disease.

The northwest scrubland is similar in landscape and climate to the northeast thornbush plains. The Kulal mountain range dominates the region. Although Lake Turkana is also located here, no major population centers line its shores.

The fourth region, the southwest highlands, forms a plateau bisected by the Great Rift Valley. More than three-quarters of the population lives in this most fertile part of the country, where the average rainfall exceeds 30 inches (760 millimeters) per year, the climate is mild, and the land is covered with thick grass and forests.

Kenyan village women often carry heavy loads atop their heads

The foothills of most of Kenya's magnificent mountain ranges originate here. Mount Kenya, Mount Elgon, and the Aberdare Mountains rise to more than 17,000 feet (5,100 meters).

Land of Mountains

Although most of Kenya is a grassy plateau, many magnificent volcanic peaks enhance the landscape. The most impressive of these is Mount Kenya, located 80 miles (128 kilometers) northeast of Nairobi. At 17,058 feet (5,199 meters), Mount Kenya is the highest mountain in Kenya and the second-highest peak in Africa. Although it sits on the equator, it is covered with snow and glaciers. The country takes its name from a tribal word for this peak, Kere-Nyaga (mountain of whiteness).

Kenya's second-highest mountain is Mount Elgon, located on the Kenya-Uganda border northeast of Lake Victoria. This mountain reaches 14,178 feet (4,321 meters), and although it is not high enough to be covered with snow year-round, blizzards ravage its summit during the winter months.

Kenya's largest mountain group, the Aberdare range, begins north of Nairobi and extends southward for more than 100 miles (161 kilometers). Smaller mountain ranges include the Kulal Mountains in northwestern Kenya, which reach 9,203 feet (2,805 meters) at Mount Nyiru, and the Teita Hills in the southeast.

Lakes and Rivers

Kenya's lakes are located in the Rift Valley. Lake Turkana in the northwest scrublands is about 180 miles (290 kilometers) in area

Lake Magadi, south of Nairobi, is a plentiful source of fish even though it is one of Kenya's smallest lakes

and stretches beyond the Ethiopian border. Vast fishing reserves make this lake important to Kenya's economy. Called Lake Rudolf by the British, it was given its African name after Kenya gained its independence.

Southwestern Kenya contains a portion of Lake Victoria, the largest lake in Africa. Uganda and Tanzania also share the lake, and the three nations use it for commercial shipping. Other large lakes in the Rift Valley include Lake Nakuru and Lake Naivasha. Smaller lakes, which the Kenyans use for fishing, include Lake Baringo in west-central Kenya and Lake Magadi, south of Nairobi. Tiny, shallow

A windmill on Lake Victoria supplies water energy to villages in Kenya

lakes in the countryside provide homes for large colonies of flamingos and other birds.

Kenya has three important rivers: the Tana, the Turkwel, and the Athi. The largest, the Tana, flows from the Indian Ocean to Mount Kenya. The Turkwel flows from Lake Turkana in the north to Lake Victoria in the south. The Athi River, located in southeastern Kenya, flows south from Nairobi through the Tsavo National Park game preserve near the Tanzania border. In the center of the game preserve, the Athi splits into two rivers: the Tsano River, which runs westward into Tanzania, and the Galana River, which flows to the Indian Ocean.

A Temperate Climate

Even though Kenya is located on the equator, its climate is mild because of cool breezes that blow inland from the Indian Ocean. The average temperature is 79° Fahrenheit (26° Centigrade). Kenya has only two seasons, summer and winter, and the difference in temperature is only about 6° F (3° C). At high altitudes, an afternoon temperature of 86° F (30° C) can drop to an overnight low of 50° F (10° C). In the mountains, temperatures drop by about 5° F (3° C) with every 1,000-foot (300-meter) increase in altitude.

Kenya has two rainy seasons: a period of heavy rain from March through May and a period of milder rain from mid-October to December. Because of the intense East African sunshine, however, rainwater quickly evaporates and droughts can occur in sections of Kenya that receive more than 30 inches (750 millimeters) of rain annually.

Plant and Animal Life

Plants and flowers thrive in Kenya. In the highlands, thick forests of evergreens are interspersed with wide expanses of short grasses. In and around Nairobi, flat-topped trees and tall grasses grow. In dry northern Kenya, only desert scrub survives, whereas in the coastal belt, tall, thick bushes alternate with small forests and open glades. Coconut palms and mangroves also flourish along the coast.

A variety of vegetation covers the slopes of Kenya's mountains. Forests of beautiful trees surround their bases. Then, at about 8,000 feet (2,425 meters), the forests give way to belts of thick bamboo. Above the bamboo sections grow clumps of twisted trees and a variety of orchids, fruits, and ferns. At about 11,000 feet (3,330 meters), this lush vegetation is replaced by an open wasteland where only the hardiest plants survive. At altitudes of more than 15,000 feet (4,545 meters), snow and ice cover the mountain peaks, and the only signs of life are birds of prey that swoop down from their icy perches to hunt animals at lower elevations.

Many exotic animals populate Kenya. In the dry thornbush plains, lions, cheetahs, leopards, and wild dogs roam, although their numbers vary depending upon the migrations of the herds. Elephants, buffalo, and rhinoceroses populate the open country and the mountain forests, and huge herds of zebras, antelope, and gazelles inhabit the coastal plains. Crocodiles and hippopotamuses live in the large rivers. Baboons roam freely, although monkeys—including the colobus variety—limit their homes to the forests. In the late 18th and early 19th centuries, Europeans and Americans came to hunt these exotic creatures. Today, they observe only.

17

Water from lakes is piped even to remote villages in Kenya

Elephant herds roam the open country and mountain forests of Kenya, where they are protected by law from hunters

Kenya is also home to many reptiles and birds. Snakes such as the venomous cobra, the mamba, the harmless puff adder (also called the hognose snake), and the deadly python live in the grasslands and along lakes and rivers. Exotic and graceful birds—including ostriches, flamingos, gazelles, storks, eagles, vultures, pelicans, weavers, and hornbills—also thrive within Kenya's borders. Herons, ibis, and ducks abound along the lakes.

Kenyan warriors used feathers, pelts, and tortoise shells for gear

A History of Immigration

Kenya's story begins long before recorded history. Scientists have found the bones and stone tools of intelligent protohumans who occupied Kenya more than 2 million years B.C. After these peoples died out, a number of others came to East Africa. The Cushitic, Bantu, and Nilotic peoples migrated to Kenya from other parts of Africa around 400 B.C. Arab traders from northern Africa and the Arabian peninsula arrived in the 8th century A.D., turning the quiet East African coast into a bustling trading center. While Africa was still a dark mystery to the European world, Kenya was a thriving nation.

At this time, Kenya's inhabitants were members of not one ethnic group but a variety of tribes. Each of these tribes had its own culture, language, religion, and customs. Tribal territories were marked by boundaries similar to those between nations. Each tribe hunted and grew crops on its own lands, and there was little need for interaction between tribes.

After the Arabs arrived, however, communication between tribes became necessary for trading purposes, and a *lingua franca* (a common language for the purposes of commerce) developed. This language, called Swahili, was a combination of Bantu (the most

21

Each tribe in Kenya has its own customs of body ornamentation

widely used African language) and Arabic. Through the use of Swahili, Kenya's diverse tribes began to interact with one another.

By the early 15th century, a Swahili culture—a mixture of African and Arab customs and beliefs—had developed in the urban commercial centers of Pate, Malindi, and Mombasa. When Portuguese explorer Vasco da Gama sailed into East Africa in the 1480s, he was astounded by the fabulous wealth of the trading centers. He sent word back to Europe that there were riches to be had, and soon Portuguese explorers invaded East Africa.

The Portuguese attacked many East African settlements. Although the Arabs fought against the invaders, they were overcome by the strength of the Portuguese navy, and in 1498 Portugal conquered Mombasa. The Portuguese built a large fortress, Fort Jesus, at the entrance to Mombasa's harbor.

For the next 250 years, fighting continued between the Arabs and the Portuguese. In the middle of the 17th century, Portugal's power began to decline, and in 1698, the Arabs captured Fort Jesus. By 1740, the Arabs had succeeded in driving the Portuguese from East Africa, and Oman, an Arab country on the southern tip of the Arabian peninsula, had control of Kenya.

During the mid-1800s, explorers and missionaries flocked to East Africa. In 1848, a British missionary discovered Mount Kilimanjaro in Tanzania, and in 1849, German missionary Ludwig Krapf became the first white man to see Mount Kenya.

When news of these wonders reached the West, European interest in Africa accelerated. European nations began proclaiming their sovereignty over East African territory. While Germany was taking over Tanzania, a private British firm was buying up Oman's landholdings in Kenya. In 1895, the British government took over the company's interests and proclaimed Kenya's interior—as far west as Lake Naivasha—a British protectorate (dependent state). In 1902, the protectorate was extended to the Uganda border, and all of Kenya—except for a coastal strip—became part of the British Empire.

Under British Rule

The British wanted Kenya for one reason: to gain access to the fertile land around Lake Victoria on the Kenya-Uganda border. By

1900, Uganda had also become a British protectorate, and in December 1895, Britain began building the Uganda Railway, a line that was to link Kenya's ports with the fertile Ugandan interior and promote the development of East Africa's economic resources. Under the direction of British Prime Minister Lord Salisbury, the first locomotive reached the town of Kismu on Lake Victoria in December 1901. By 1903, the railway was completed.

A freight train climbing Kenya's Rift Valley is part of the line built by the British to transport economic resources in East Africa

In order to begin exploiting Kenya's natural resources, the British government encouraged European settlers to immigrate to the country's fertile highlands at the western end of the railway line. The response to this invitation was greater than the government expected. Thousands of British settlers poured into Africa, and native Kenyans watched as the colonists overran their ancestral lands.

To make way for the colonists, the goverment sent tribespeople to reservations far from their traditional homelands. Many tribes did not resist. Even the Maasai, considered the most warlike tribesmen, went peacefully to their reservation. But the members of Kenya's largest and most powerful tribe, the Kikuyu, felt that the British had invaded their territory. They viewed land as a sacred commodity and resented British attempts to take over tribal grounds. The Kikuyu attacked British settlements and reclaimed some of their land. Eventually, however, the British military subdued the Kikuyu, and they lost their ancestral lands.

The Farm Economy

By the early 1900s, the British colonists had penetrated deep into Kenya and had settled in the fertile area around the Great Rift Valley. They began developing large agricultural plantations to grow coffee and tea. After the farms were completed, the settlers found that they needed a huge labor force to work the plantations.

The settlers assumed that native Kenyans would volunteer to work the fields. They were wrong. The Africans felt no obligation to work for those who had taken over their territories. Even tribes that had not rebelled against the British now refused to work in the settlements. In response, the territorial government created mandatory labor laws, forcing native Kenyans to work for low wages on colonial farms.

The British settlers prospered as a result of the inexpensive native labor. Soon, the British government began establishing schools and government councils for the settlers. However, the British ig-

The wife of a British settler supervises young native workers on her husband's plantation in colonial Kenya

This thatch-roofed, stone cottage is typical of the houses British colonists built on their plantations in Kenya

nored the concerns of native Africans. They failed to provide tribespeople with a school system and did not grant them representation in the legislature. Christian missionaries began asserting authority over native practices and forbade a number of tribal rituals. Furthermore, the British kept native Africans from making economic gains by making it illegal for them to grow coffee, a major cash crop. The only work the British allowed Africans to do was low-paying labor on white plantations.

The Rise of Nationalism

In the 1920s, Kenya's native people began to rebel against repressive British rule. The Kikuyu tribe, which had long been the most active in opposing the British, was the first to organize. Prominent Kikuyu tribesman Harry Thuku established the Young Kikuyu Association and began inciting tribespeople to defy British laws. He urged them to refuse to work on plantations and to destroy the identification cards that the British forced all native people to carry.

Thuku's efforts were effective, and the British began to fear his power. In 1922, they arrested him, charging that he was "dangerous to peace and good order." After his arrest, a crowd of supporters gathered outside the prison demanding his release. British police opened fire, and 25 Africans, including 4 women and a small child, were killed. This incident, which became known as the Nairobi Massacre, caused a worldwide reaction against the British, but the settlers were undaunted. The repressive policies continued, and soon native organizations were springing up all over the country to protest the British presence.

For the next two decades, the native people continued to fight the British, but with limited success. In the early 1940s, however, native leaders took their campaign for freedom to European capi-

Kenyan tribesmen pose for a formal portrait, taken in the 1920s

tals, and foreign pressure against Britain increased. By 1944, Britain was forced to make Kenya the first African territory with a tribal representative in its legislature. By 1951, eight native Africans occupied seats in the Kenyan legislature. Still, many Africans were dissatisfied with both their representation in government and their economic situation. As high unemployment and economic exploitation by European settlers continued, resentment among Kenya's Africans grew.

The Mau Mau Rebellion

In the late 1940s, African frustration exploded in scattered incidents of violence against settlers. In the early 1950s, this violence increased, and a full-scale rebellion rocked Kenya. The British blamed this uprising, known as the Mau Mau Rebellion, on the Kikuyu tribe, whose opposition to British domination had been the most vocal. Soon, the settlers began attributing every act of violence in Kenya to the Kikuyu. In October 1952, the British declared a state of emergency in Kenya, and on October 21, Kenya's governor arrested Jomo Kenyatta, a Kikuyu leader, and charged him with instigating the uprising. Kenyatta was sentenced to seven years in prison.

The arrest of Jomo Kenyatta proved to be a mistake. He was the most visible and well-respected of Kenya's African leaders, and

Kenya's rebellion against British domination returned the nation to its native people

violence increased rather than declined after he was imprisoned. By 1959, it was clear that British domination of Kenya could not continue. In 1960, as a result of a conference held in London, Britain granted Kenya's Africans majority rule. Two groups, the Kenya African National Union (KANU) and the Kenya African Democratic Union (KADU), were to lead Kenya to independence.

Unfortunately, tribal disputes sparked conflict between the two groups. KANU was comprised mostly of members from the Kikuyu and Luo tribes, whereas KADU had the support of only the smaller tribes. In 1962, another London conference brought both parties together and convinced them to form a coalition to ensure full self-government for Kenya. In 1963, KADU joined KANU, and KANU's leaders became the heads of Kenya's government.

On December 12, 1963, Kenya was granted independence. Jomo Kenyatta, who after his release from prison in 1961 had replaced Tom Mboya as KANU's leader, became the country's first prime minister. When Kenya held free elections in 1964, Kenyatta became president.

The Notable President

For more than 40 years, Jomo Kenyatta had led the fight for Kenyan independence. Educated by the British but loyal to his Kikuyu people, he used his knowledge of the white man's world and his understanding of the African people to unite a nation against the inhumanities of colonization.

Kenyatta was born Kamau wa Ngengi (Kamau, son of Ngengi) in Ichaweri, Kenya, in the 1890s. The son of a Kikuyu farmer, he

31

first encountered the Europeans who were colonizing Kenya when he was ten years old and seriously ill with a leg infection. His parents, desperate to cure him after the tribal doctor had failed, took him to the British mission of Fort Hall, about 30 miles (48 kilometers) from his village. There, white doctors healed his infection and saved his life.

When he returned to Ichaweri, Kamau could not forget the mission and all the fascinating things he had seen there. As soon as he had fully recovered from his illness, he ran away from his village, back to Fort Hall. For the next three years, he attended the British mission school. By the time he was 13, he could speak, read, and write English as though it were his native tongue.

When he was 14, Kamau returned to his village to be initiated as an adult Kikuyu. He married and set up a home, but he never forgot what he had learned at the mission. After a few years, he returned to Fort Hall, where he studied math, learned to speak Swahili, and was baptized a Christian by the missionaries. The missionaries even gave him a new name: Johnstone Kamau.

Kamau continued to work and study at the mission until 1924, when the Kikuyu leader Chief Kioi brought suit against the British for usurping tribal lands. The chief asked the educated Kamau to assist him in presenting his position to the court at Nairobi. Although the Kikuyu lost their case, the public attention that the case received marked the beginning of Johnstone Kamau's career as a leader in African politics.

In 1920, at the age of about 26, Kamau moved to Nairobi and changed his name to Kenyatta, the Kikuyu word for the beaded belt that all Kikuyu men wear. For two years he ignored politics, but in 1922 he joined the newly formed East African Association (EAA). He quickly rose to a position of power in the EAA, and in 1928 he became secretary of the group, which had changed its name to the Kikuyu Central Organization.

In 1929, Kenyatta represented the organization on a trip to London, and in 1931 he took up residence in England. He spent the next two decades traveling around Europe, presenting the African position to anyone who would listen. In 1938, he wrote *Fac-*

Kenyatta wears a monkey skin robe presented by the Kikuyus

ing Mount Kenya, a book that brought the plight of native Africans to the attention of the Western world. In 1945, he and the great black-American educator Dr. W.E.B. Du Bois helped organize the Manchester Pan-African Congress, the first effort to unite the leaders of Britain's many African colonies.

In 1946, Kenyatta—who had dropped the British name Johnstone in favor of "Jomo," a name he coined—returned to Kenya for the first time in 17 years. Now a noted leader in the African rights movement, Kenyatta became the president of the New Kenya African Union in 1947. When the Mau Mau uprising began in 1952, the British arrested Kenyatta and sentenced him to seven years in prison. His arrest only fueled the fire of African independence, and two years after his release from prison, British rule ended.

In 1964, Kenyatta became president of Kenya. He united his people under the slogan *Harambee*, Swahili for "pull together." He stopped the feuding between the Kikuyu and Luo tribes by wearing his Kikuyu kenyatta belt around his waist and the cap of a Luo chieftain on his head. Although he accepted assistance from both Western and Communist countries, he strictly forbade Communist activities within Kenya. Nicknamed Mzee (the old man), Kenyatta retained the presidency until his death in 1978.

Because of Kenyatta's tolerant, practical, and conservative leadership, world leaders regard today's Kenya as a stable, pro-Western country. Africa has seen much unrest in the past two decades, but under the administrations of Kenyatta and his successor, Daniel arap Moi, Kenya remains one of the most politically stable nations on the continent.

The Republic

When Kenya gained its independence in 1963, its government ratified a new constitution. Under that constitution, Kenya's government became a republic comprised of three branches: an executive branch administered by a president, a legislative branch led by a single-chambered legislature, and a judicial branch headed by the High Court (also called the Supreme Court).

Kenya's legislature is called the National Assembly. The assembly is made up of 158 members, whom the public selects in general elections. Terms of office in the legislature vary; the maximum is five years. The president appoints 12 assemblymen, in addition to

Nairobi women show the government that they support saving energy

the attorney general and the speaker, who are *ex officio* (by the nature of their office) members of the assembly.

Kenya's president has three titles: chief of state, head of government, and commander in chief of the armed forces. Although all Kenyans over the age of 18 have voting privileges, the president is not elected by the populace. Rather, he is a member of the National Assembly and is elected by his fellow assemblymen to a five-year term. The president in turn appoints his vice president and cabinet members from among the members of the assembly. All assembly members belong to Kenya's only political party, KANU.

At the head of Kenya's judicial branch is the High Court, which is comprised of a chief justice and 11 subordinate justices (known as *Puisne* judges). The president appoints all court members. The court has full jurisdiction over all civil and criminal matters and travels throughout the country, holding sessions in Nairobi, Mombasa, and Kismu. Every lawyer in Kenya has the right to appear before the High Court as well as all local and district courts.

About 3 percent of Kenyans are Muslims, and the government allows them to enforce their own religious laws. Although they are subject to the civil and criminal laws of the state, the rules of their religion—contained in the Koran, their holy book—are interpreted by Islamic courts presided over by *Kadhis* (Muslim judges). These courts have the power to mete out punishments to Muslims who break Islamic laws.

Under its first constitution, Kenya was divided into seven provinces—Coast, Central, Rift Valley, Nyanza, Western, Northeastern, and Eastern—and one independent area known as the Nairobi District. These provinces had semiautonomous governments, with the power to make laws concerning education, health care, law enforcement, and civil service. Amendments to the constitution have greatly reduced the powers of the provincial governments, however, and today, a commissioner appointed by the president governs each province. A city council governs the Nairobi District.

Kenya belongs to a number of international and inter-African organizations. After gaining its independence in 1963, it became a member of the United Nations, and it has received assistance from U.N. agencies, such as the World Health Organization and the Food and Agriculture Organization.

Kenya also belongs to the Commonwealth of Nations, an association headed by Great Britain. The commonwealth grants memberships to nations that were part of the old British Empire and wish to maintain good relations with Britain. These nations consult one another on economic, educational, scientific, financial, and military matters.

Kenya's capital city, Nairobi, is governed by its own council

37

The strong, stable government of Kenya has united its people

Two important African associations count Kenya as a member. The country was a founder of the Organization of African Unity (OAU), a group dedicated to promoting African progress and co-operation. With neighboring Uganda and Tanzania, Kenya has formed the East African Common Services Organization, which provides economic and educational services to the citizens of member nations.

Independent Kenya has a record of political stability that is unmatched in Africa. It has never had a civil war or a coup d'etat. Because of this stability, its people have not suffered greatly from the scourge of famine that has devastated many of its neighbors. Kenya has stayed the course initiated by Jomo Kenyatta and has maintained a position of cooperation and strength in dealing with the West and with its African neighbors.

A Diverse People

Kenya's inhabitants belong to many races. Anthropologists believe that more than 300 different tribes live in East Africa. Each of these tribes is like a nation unto itself, with its own customs, traditions, and culture. Kenya is also a melting pot of non-African peoples, with large communities of Europeans, Arabs, Indians, Goans (people from Goa in western India), Pakistanis, and Asians. Although

Native Kenyans adapt to modern ways at a textile factory in Mombasa

Kenya is united under one flag and one leader, it is actually a nation of nations.

Kenya's people practice a number of religions. Today, only 28 percent of Kenyans are members of the tribal cults that once were the dominant religion. The most common of these native creeds center on the worship of tribal forefathers and faith in Ngai, the High God. Belief in magic, witches, and sorcerers is still widespread among native Kenyans.

A full 38 percent of the population is Protestant, largely because of the efforts of European missionaries. Catholic missionaries are also active in Kenya and have managed to convert 28 percent of the population. Although Christian missions still operate in Kenya, many African separatist churches have broken away from the missions.

Many of the tribes in Kenya's northern deserts and coastal regions are Muslim, and Islam is still spreading. In the past decade, Kenya's Muslim population has doubled, increasing from 3 to 6 percent.

The first non-Africans to inhabit Kenya were Arab traders who arrived in the 8th century. After the Kenya-Uganda railroad was constructed in the early 20th century, North African Arabs migrated to Kenya and settled in Mombasa and Nairobi. Many of the Arabs who live in Kenya's cities are merchants, whereas those who live in the countryside often work on coconut plantations.

Indians, Pakistanis, and Goans are the largest immigrant groups. Indians and Pakistanis comprise the main commercial and artisan classes throughout Kenya. Most Goans work in government and clerical services as well as in the tailoring industry.

Europeans from Britain, France, and Germany form another large group. Concentrated in the fertile farmland of the highlands and in Nairobi, Kenya's European population enjoys a great economic advantage. Europeans still control most of Kenya's agriculture, and they are also involved in professional, technical, and commercial employment and public services.

Of Kenya's 19,362,000 inhabitants, slightly more than half—10,733,202—are Africans. Kenya's African peoples fall into three broad ethno-linguistic groups: the Bantu-speaking peoples, including the Kikuyu, the Kamba, and the Meru; the Nilotic peoples, such as the Luo; and the Nilo-Hamitic peoples, including the Maasai, the

Kenyan women grow crops and make pottery to help support the family

Kingsigi, the Turkana, and the Nandi. Although the European influence has affected many tribes, native Kenyans have struggled to retain their traditional ways of life.

The Kikuyu

Kenya's largest ethnic group, the Kikuyu, comprises 16 percent of the country's population. Most of Kenya's 3.2 million Kikuyu inhabit the Central Province. The country's history is closely tied to the history of these farming people, whose attachment to their land gave them the determination to fight British oppression.

The Kikuyu's early history revolved around searching for—and fighting over—land. Long before the Europeans arrived, the

This rural market in Kenya sells handicrafts and factory-made goods

Kikuyu were seasoned veterans of land disputes. The most frequent of these occurred between the Kikuyu and the Nderobo and Maasai tribes. When conflicts arose with the Nderobo, the Kikuyu used discussion and treaty to settle them. But with the warlike Maasai, the Kikuyu often resorted to bloodshed. After the arrival of the British, however, the tribe used its energies to secure tribal lands against British ownership.

Kikuyu society places tremendous emphasis on the family unit, called the *nyumba*. Strict traditions govern family life. For instance, work is divided along gender lines. In addition to taking care of children and the home, women plant, cultivate, and harvest small crops and create pottery and baskets—known as *kiondo*—that can be sold to help support the family. Men, on the other hand, care for herds, plant major crops, and protect tribal lands.

Kikuyu traditionally have large families, because the larger the family, the larger the plot of land it can farm. Although much has changed in Kenya over the past century, Kikuyu beliefs and customs remain linked to their reverence for a large and close-knit family life.

In addition to the family, the Kikuyu also have a special reverence for the "age set," a group made up of all Kikuyu born in the same year. Members of an age set are expected to protect, teach, and be loyal to one another. When they reach the age of about 18, they undergo a group ceremony that initiates them into adulthood. During the coming-of-age ritual, the young Kikuyu have their ears pierced, their heads shaved, and their faces marked with white earth.

Young herders in Kenya relax while tending their tribe's cattle

After initiation, Kikuyu are considered adults and may marry. Marriage is entered into only after much discussion among the elders of the tribe. When a match has been made, the groom's father pays a dowry—usually livestock—to the bride's family. For instance, when Jomo Kenyatta married, his father gave the bride's parents 34 sheep in payment.

The Kikuyu religion revolves around belief in Ngai, a god whom the Maasai and other Kenyan tribes also worship. Ngai is believed to live atop Mount Kenya, and tribespeople often make offerings at the base of the towering mountain to show reverence for their god.

The music and dance of the Kikuyu are much simpler than those of other tribes. The instrument they use most is the picture rattle, or *gicandi*—a hollowed gourd filled with hard seeds and decorated to depict the travels of the person playing it. For generations, Kikuyu have passed down the songs of gicandi minstrels, and many young Kikuyu find the ancient songs difficult to understand.

The modernization of Kenya has altered Kikuyu life. Many tribesmen have left farming and taken jobs in government and business. Since Kenya gained its independence, its leaders have been Kikuyu, which is not surprising, as they have traditionally had an intricate system of self-government. Despite all the changes that have taken place in their country over the past century, the Kikuyu

Musicians playing ancestral instruments attract a crowd in Mombasa

retain a reverence for the land and a pride in their heritage. Were it not for the brave Kikuyu, Kenya might still be under British domination.

The Luhya People

Another large ethnic group is that of the Luhya people, who live north of Lake Victoria in the Western Province. A farming tribe of more than 2.1 million people, it is noted for its handicrafts and unique tribal rituals. Like the Kikuyu, the Luhya separate male and

This young Kenyan has traded in his traditional tribal clothing for simpler everyday attire

female work roles. Luhya women make distinctive pottery and baskets decorated with intricate tribal designs. Luhya men farm the land.

The Luhya have elaborate music and dance rituals. Their tribe is one of the few in Kenya whose dancers still use masks. In addition, they use great wicker shields and a wide range of instruments, such as flutes, horns, drums, fiddles, the eight-stringed lyre, and the *mlele*—an instrument that can produce an amazing range of notes.

The Luo and the Kisii Peoples

The Luo and Kisii tribes inhabit the Nyanza Province. Although the Luo are farmers, they are less prosperous than other tribespeople because they live in western Nyanza, which has rocky soil and slight rainfall. When rain does fall in this region, it tends to fall in spurts, and the Luo sometimes face both flood and drought within a matter of months.

Traditionally, the Luo measured wealth in terms of cattle and land, but this is less true today. Modern Luo rely on dairy farming and fishing for their livelihood. The preparation of fish, which is either cooked, roasted whole, or smoked and dried, is an important part of Luo ritual.

Of all of Kenya's ethnic groups, the Luo has the most decorative tribal clothing. Traditional Luo dress includes ornate body ornaments and intricate headdresses made of feathers, metal, and hippo tusks. The Luo most often play their music on the lyre, a harp-like instrument.

The sixth-most populous group in Kenya is that of the Kisii, who inhabit fertile eastern Nyanza. The Kisii (or Gusii, as they are sometimes called) are Bantu-speaking people who live in many parts of northern Africa. As is the Bantu tradition, they are experts in both agriculture and iron making. Many tribes once used as currency twisted iron bars known as Kisii pennies.

The Kisii are mystical people who still perform many ancient healing rituals. For example, they practice *trepanning* (cutting a

A Luo woman wears body ornaments for which her tribe is noted

Many tribal groups in Kenya still practice ancient healing rituals

hole in the skull), which they believe releases sickness, mental illness, or evil spirits from the body. The Kisii also cure the sick using herbal medicines made from tree bark and other natural materials.

The Kalenjin and the Turkana Peoples

The Great Rift Valley is the home of the Kalenjin, the Turkana, and the Maasai peoples. About half of the valley's 3.7 million inhabitants are Kalenjin, a group encompassing the Nandi, Kipsigis, Turgen, Elgeyo, Marakwet, and Pokot tribes.

The Kalenjin live in the highlands, and like most of Kenya's tribal peoples, they are farmers. At one time, they were noted for their practice of herbal medicine performed by female doctors. Now, however, they frown upon herbal medicine, witchcraft, and other mystical rites.

The Turkana people inhabit an inhospitable area of the Rift Valley west of Lake Turkana. Although they are primarily a pastoral people, they also hunt, gather honey, and fish. Because they inhabit a harsh, dry area of Kenya, the Turkana must constantly wander in search of better grazing land for their herds. As a result, they live in simple homes that can be easily moved. Their principal source of wealth is the camel, which provides them with transportation as well as milk.

The Maasai

Although there are only 200,000 Maasai people in Kenya—just 1 percent of the population—the tribe is famous for its warriors. The word Maasai comes from "Maa," the name of the unwritten language they speak. Several different groups of Maasai live in East Africa, and each has its own name, leaders, dialect, and style of dress. The Kenyan Maasai, for instance, are called the Ilpurko people and dress in short orange or blue tunics. The tribe's nomadic tendencies, fascinating folklore, and colorful dress have fostered many romantic legends and have had a tremendous impact on the way Westerners view Africans.

The Maasai are a herding people, and reverence for cattle forms the basis of their culture. The only thing more important to the Maasai than their herds is their children. In fact, the traditional greeting of one Maasai to another is "Keserian ingera? Keserian

Famed warriors, Maasai in Kenya no longer fight battles but are equally renowned for their devotion to their children and cattle

ingishu?" which means, "How are the children? How are the cattle?" If a Maasai commits a crime against the tribe, he must pay a cattle fine.

The Maasai is perhaps best known as East Africa's greatest warrior tribe, and members still perform warrior rituals, although few Maasai wars have occurred in the past century. Although it is now illegal, young Maasai still participate in the ritual lion hunt. Maasai warriors consider spearing a lion the high point of their life. The warrior who kills the lion claims the lion's tail and mane, and his fellow warriors call out his family name in triumph.

The young warriors wear headdresses of ostrich or eagle feathers and strap metal belts to their thighs. After the hunt, the men

These Kenyans are playing **dodoi***, a game that is popular in Africa*

head home, where a long celebration—and young Maasai women—await the victorious warrior. The most beautiful woman wins his affections. A woman's beauty is determined by the craftsmanship of the necklaces she has made for herself.

The Maasai people are known among other tribes as the creators of *dodoi*, a game of skill played with bowls of seeds or pebbles. The game is popular throughout Africa under a variety of names; in Senegal it is known as *ouri*, in Togo as *aju*, and in Zaire as *mankala*.

Although Kenya's Maasai still perform some of their ancient rites and rituals, it is not unusual to see them shopping in Nairobi dressed in European-style clothes. But regardless of the changes that take place among the Maasai in the future, they will remain people of tradition and romance.

The Kamba, the Embu, the Mbere, and the Meru

The Eastern Province is inhabited by the Kamba, the Embu, the Mbere, and the Meru. The Embu and the Mbere have many of the same beliefs and customs as the Kikuyu. The Embu, who inhabit the rich land of the southeast slopes of Mount Kenya, grow coffee and tea. The Mbere people have traditionally raised cattle.

The Kamba—who number about 1.75 million—are a Bantu-speaking people. At one time they were herders, but they have since turned to agriculture and trade for their livelihood. They are known for their crafts, particularly metal work, wood carving, and the creation of hand-carved, three-legged stools.

Eastern Province Kenyans are known for elaborate wood carvings

Kamba dance rituals are perhaps the most sensational of all of Kenya's tribal dances. In recent years, traditional dances have added Western elements, combining military whistle-blowing and drill-like movements with acrobatics, somersaults, and leaping, all choreographed to ancient rhythms.

The Meru, who form Kenya's seventh-largest group, inhabit the region to the east and northeast of Mount Kenya. They earn their living by cultivating *miraa*, a stimulant favored by Kenya's coastal residents.

The Somalis

Kenya's Northeastern Province is inhabited by the Somalis, an Islamic people from Somalia, north of Kenya. Because they are Muslims, their society is very strict and male-dominated. When a woman marries, she can expect to be one of up to four wives. When a divorce occurs, the father retains custody of all the male children, and the mother must raise all the female children.

The harsh northeastern climate dictates a nomadic existence for the Somalis. They are constantly on the move and keep material possessions to a minimum. Their diet is largely vegetarian; they eat meat only during special ceremonies. The Somalis often purchase grains from traders to supplement their diet.

Kenyans harvest pyrethrum, a native plant used to make insecticide

Village Life

Although Kenya now has several large, bustling cities, more than 90 percent of native Africans still live in small, remote villages. Despite the modernization of Kenya's urban centers, life in small, country towns remains much as it has for centuries.

Kenya's land has long been divided along tribal lines. For example, Kikuyu live in the Central Province, Luhya in the Western Province, and Luo in the Nyanza. Similarly, most villages are inhabited by members of only one tribe. Because of this, village life varies greatly. Just as each tribe has its own language, customs, and culture, each village has its own form of housing, type of economy, and way of life.

Today, most Kenyans still live in small, remote villages

This mud, wood, and grass house is one of many native types

The shape and size of a village dwelling varies according to tribal traditions and available building materials. Most homes are made of natural materials found in the countryside: trees, long grasses, and mud. But there are as many varieties of homes as there are Kenyan tribes: *zaramo* houses, rectangular in shape, are made of grass; *rundi* houses are shaped like round beehives and are constructed of reeds bound together with bark; *chagga* houses are built from sticks and resemble Indian wigwams; and *nyamwezi* huts resemble thatched circus tents.

Because of the busy daily routine of most villagers, only those who are ill stay indoors, and most Kenyans consider their houses only as places to sleep and to prepare meals. Because of this, most village huts are small and stark. Floors are made of mud or packed dirt, and the only light is the dim glow of the cooking fire. The only pieces of furniture are straw or reed mats used as bedding.

57

Most huts contain only one room, although Maasai houses are divided into four compartments: a sleeping area for the women, quarters for the children, a private section for the husband, and a cooking and dining area. In addition to permanent dwellings, some tribes build temporary shelters, called *hides*, where villagers can dwell while watching over their crops. Hides also provide a resting place during the working day.

Most work centers around cultivating food. Villagers rise at dawn to tend to their daily vegetable farming. Crops include maize (also known as Indian corn), sorghum, millet, potatoes, and rice. Another common village occupation is cattle-raising. In the coastal villages along the shallow waters of the Indian Ocean, the primary food is fish, and the chief occupation of village men is fishing. The fishermen use small boats known as *ngalawa* to reach fertile, off-shore fishing grounds. They carve the ngalawa from wood, in a variety of sizes. Some are only big enough to hold two people; others are large enough to carry ten.

Like most Kenyan villagers, this man harvests corn by hand

Open-air markets such as this one are found in every Kenyan village

Every village has an open-air market—usually located in the center of town—where villagers can sell their wares. Items such as fruits and vegetables, handicrafts, jewelry, and clothing are set out on the ground to be inspected by prospective buyers. Often, nomadic traders bring their wares to the village market.

Despite the many changes that the 20th century has brought to Kenya, life in the villages retains its charm and simplicity. However, village life will inevitably change as the country continues to grow.

Kenya's Cities

Although the majority of Kenya's people still lives in the country-side, its urban population is growing rapidly. In the past decade, the number of city-dwellers has increased from fewer than 1 million to almost 5 million people. The population of Nairobi, the capital city, more than doubled in a ten-year period. Although this has caused an increase in unemployment and poverty, Nairobi remains the most prosperous city in Kenya.

In the early 1900s, Nairobi emerged as a center for commerce

Nairobi takes its name from a Maasai word meaning "place of cool waters." When British settlers arrived in the late 1800s, Nairobi was a small village inhabited by Maasai tribesmen. Over the next century, it became the hub of British operations in East Africa. Today, it is the commercial center of all of East Africa. Its industrial centers and banking facilities are the largest in the region, and people from all over the world live and work in Nairobi.

Elegant shops, boutiques, and restaurants abound in downtown Nairobi. Tourists and wealthy Nairobians alike frequent exclusive stores such as Roland Ward's, which features safari boots, ebony wood carvings, precious gemstones, and other African specialties. Nairobi's restaurants serve an array of international fare, although many visitors prefer to sample traditional Kenyan food at bistros such as the African Heritage Café.

Nairobi's cultural tastes are also sophisticated. The National Museum of Nairobi, located off of the Uhuru Highway, has a fine collection of fossils and early human remains. Kenya's leading art gallery, Gallery Watatu, features the work of leading artists from Kenya and other African countries. Other galleries, such as Studio 68, contain African artifacts, clothing, and artwork.

As Kenya's cultural center, Nairobi has many dramatic and film theaters. At the Donovan Maule Theatre, British actors perform productions of popular London plays. The Kenya National Theatre features performances by local and international artists, and the French Cultural Center shows a variety of French films.

The Kenyatta International Conference Center and the Cooperative Bank Building distinguish the city's modern skyline. Other

Although Nairobi is the largest commercial center in East Africa, parks, arboretums, and gardens still flourish there

62

buildings of interest include the Law Courts, City Hall, the National Assembly Building, the University of Nairobi, the Roman Catholic Cathedral, All Saints Cathedral, Jamia Mosque, and the McMillan Library. A number of modern resort hotels also fill the city.

Like the rest of Kenya, Nairobi abounds with natural wonders. It has been nicknamed the City of Flowers because its streets are lined with hibiscus, oleander, and blossoming jacaranda trees. The city park features a beautiful display of plants and flowers. The Nairobi Arboretum houses a variety of trees, and Snake Park has more than 200 species of snakes.

Although life in Nairobi is fast and complicated by Kenyan standards, the pace is actually leisurely when compared to an American or European city. There are still shoeshine stands on the corners, and Nairobians can still buy fresh meats and fruits at the Municipal Market, the city's answer to the open-air markets of the country villages.

Mombasa, Malindi, and Lamu

Kenya has 300 miles (480 kilometers) of coastline along the Indian Ocean. The natural seaports and sun-drenched beaches of these coastal areas have attracted foreigners since Arab traders arrived in the 8th century. Today, three ancient coastal cities—Mombasa, Malindi, and Lamu—are thriving trading ports and tourist resorts.

Mombasa, Kenya's second-largest city and largest seaport, is located on an island near the country's southern coast. Its population of Arabs, Portuguese, and Indians reflects its history. Traders from North Africa and Arabia built a settlement there in the 8th century. In the late 1400s, Portuguese sailors conquered the city. Although Portugal eventually lost control of Mombasa, many Portuguese settled in the area. In the late 19th and early 20th centuries, when Great Britain ruled Kenya, people from British-controlled India came to Mombasa to work on construction projects. Its varied population gives Mombasa a unique cultural flavor.

Ancient Muslim architecture, believed to date back to the 8th century, lines the streets of Mombasa's quaint Old Town section. In order to preserve these old buildings, no cars are permitted along the narrow streets and alleyways. Overlooking Old Town is

Mombasa was the site of much new construction in the early 1900s

Fort Jesus, built by the Portuguese when they conquered Mombasa in the 15th century. The fortress is now a museum.

Mombasa has two distinct harbors. Small craft still use its old harbor, which for centuries served as a trading port. The new harbor, called Kilindini, is equipped with modern refueling facilities and is deep enough to accommodate the supertankers that bring crude oil to Kenya's refineries.

Mombasa's historic sites and coastal location have recently begun to attract many European vacationers. Modern resort hotels dot the northern and southern ends of the island, and tourist shops

This cathedral is one of Mombasa's many preserved historical sites

carry silks, jewelry, *saris* (Indian robes), and antiques reminiscent of the treasures of Zanzibar. But because the city itself has no beaches, sun worshippers must travel to mainland beaches by way of the new Makupa Causeway.

Malindi

About 77 miles (123 kilometers) north of Mombasa is Malindi, a popular vacation area. Its many resort hotels attract visitors from all over the world, and its beaches are the finest in Kenya. The Blue Marlin, Malindi's first beach hotel, has hosted a number of important guests, including author Ernest Hemingway, who returned there a number of times.

The town is famous for the Gedi Ruins, the remains of a 13th-century Swahili town that was abandoned in the 15th century. Set in a thick tropical forest, the well-preserved ruins provide a rare glimpse into Kenya's past.

Malindi is known as the deep-sea fishing capital of the Indian Ocean, and the waters off its shores host a variety of sea life. In addition to large game fish, such as blue marlin, a variety of tropical fish populate the waters. The Marine National Park in Malindi offers rides in glass-bottom boats, from which visitors can see beautiful coral formations and exotic aquatic creatures.

Lamu

Kenya's history comes alive in Lamu, 80 miles (128 kilometers) north of Malindi. This traditional Muslim town, located on a secluded island, has changed little in the past 200 years. Its 18th-

These Kenyans are carrying elephant tusks, prized for their ivory

century seaport and arabesque courtyards are beautiful examples of Arab-Swahili architecture.

Lamu's streets are crowded with rows of whitewashed, stucco houses. The most notable features of these traditional dwellings are their large, arched doorways, fitted with intricately carved, brass-studded, wooden doors. The island's history is preserved at the Lamu Museum, a 19th-century house displaying Swahili artifacts.

Because most of Lamu's people adhere strictly to Islamic law, life in the city remains much as it has for centuries. The city's only modern features are a movie theater, a hydroelectric plant, and one automobile (driven by a government official). Because Muslims are forbidden to drink alcohol, there are no bars, nightclubs, or other Western entertainment centers. The most common meeting place is the mosque. Although it has a population of only 9,500 people, Lamu has 31 mosques.

Most of Lamu's women obey *purdah*, the Muslim custom of secluding females from public view. They cover their faces and bodies with long, black robes called *chadors* and never allow their hair to be seen in public. Lamuan men wear flowing, white robes called *kanzus*.

Although several bridges connect the mainland to the island, they are often washed out. Most visitors reach Lamu by air, landing at its tiny airstrip. Lamu's people encourage tourism, and as a result, increasing numbers of vacationers are visiting the city. Its small hotels offer a quaint, old-world atmosphere, and shuttle buses drive vacationers to beaches at nearby Shella and Pazali Rock, where they can swim and fish.

Kenya's cities are full of contrasts, and vestiges of the traditional and the modern exist side by side. As the nation struggles toward progress, its people cling fast to their ancient traditions, and its leaders try to utilize the best of two worlds to build a strong Kenya.

Economy and Public Services

For hundreds of years, Kenya's tribespeople fed themselves through farming. But after European settlers arrived in the late-19th and early-20th centuries, many native people lost their land. Since the country gained its independence in 1963, however, native people have been granted better and larger plots of land. Today, Kenya's African farmers produce enough to feed themselves and to export agricultural goods.

Kenyan farmers harvest sisal, a fiber plant used to make rope

Processing tea is one of Kenya's most valuable industries

Kenyans have traditionally cultivated coffee, tea, and sisal, a fiber used to make rope. Recently, however, many Africans have begun raising crops that have shorter growing seasons, such as cereals and sugarcane, which they can cultivate several times a year to yield higher profits. Coffee and tea remain Kenya's two most important exports, but other crops are also becoming valuable to the economy.

Raising livestock is another source of employment for the Kenyans. Traditionally, Kenyans raised goats and sheep. When the British plantation owners arrived, they brought the science of dairy farming to Kenya. For many years, dairy farming was an almost exclusively European occupation, but it is becoming increasingly important to Africans.

Kenyan industry was born in the 1940s and 1950s, when the large number of Europeans in Kenya created a need for manufactured goods. Kenyans now work in many light industries, most notably food and beverage processing; vehicle assembly and repair; chemical manufacturing; textile, footwear, and clothing manufacturing; and metal production.

The first site of heavy industry in Kenya was the Mombasa oil refinery, built in 1961. By 1971, petroleum products had become Kenya's third most valuable export. Mombasa's modern port facilities accommodate the supertankers that bring valuable crude oil to the refinery. Other heavy industries include cement production and machine manufacturing.

Light industry such as milk-can production is growing in Kenya

The occupations of Kenya's African citizens and its European immigrants differ greatly. Most Africans still live in the countryside and support themselves by farming or raising cattle. The majority of Europeans, on the other hand, work in the urban industrial centers. Although most Europeans in Kenya have a higher standard of living than their counterparts in the United Kingdom, the average African is decidedly poorer than his Asian, Indian, or European counterpart.

Kenya's Africans have recently begun to benefit from the International Federation of Free Trade Unions. Rural workers showed their first interest in unions in 1959, when they unionized the coffee, tea, and sisal industries. Today, the Kenya Federation of Labor and the Federation of Kenya Employers represent most of Kenya's unions. The government's Labor Department has also aided workers by enforcing fair labor laws and providing employment services and assistance to both workers and employers.

The Plight of the Poor

Unemployment is still a major concern in Kenya. The rapid growth of the nation's cities has changed traditional lifestyles and caused many economic problems. Cities—flooded with rural Africans seeking work—have been unable to provide jobs and housing for all who need them. As a result, Kenya's cities are divided between the very wealthy and the very poor.

Nowhere is this more evident than in Nairobi. Its wealthiest suburb, Mathaiga, is a paradise of manicured lawns, blooming flower gardens, and colonial estates owned by moneyed Europeans. Only

A woman purchases wares from a vendor in rural Kenya

a mile from this exclusive enclave is Mathare Valley, a shantytown of makeshift huts inhabited by jobless Africans from the countryside. Many of Mathare's residents are homeless children abandoned by their unemployed parents.

Outside Nairobi in Ofafa Kariokor, the government has built housing projects for the homeless. As overpopulation and the lack of farmland have pushed more Kenyans out of the countryside and into urban areas, however, the government has had trouble dealing with the increase in poverty and homelessness. Like other developing nations, Kenya is searching for ways to provide for all of its poor.

73

Education

For centuries, tribal law and ritual determined the course of Kenya's educational system. Elders instructed native teenagers in the ways of their ethnic group, including their responsibilities to their spouses and families, tribal farming techniques, and other skills that would help them in their daily lives. Because most tribes had no written language, Kenya's native people were not literate in the traditional sense. Instead, they learned the tribe's oral tradition and the legends and lore of their people.

Western education came to Kenya in the 19th century, when the British began settling in West Africa. Christian missionaries—both Catholic and Protestant—flocked to the area to teach the children of European settlers and to spread the gospel to the native

Like most Kenyan children, this girl attends public school

people. At first, the missionaries saw no need to educate the natives in anything other than Christianity, but by the early 20th century they began to offer basic education to tribespeople and others—mostly Arabs and Indians—who lived in Kenya. They segregated schools by race, with separate facilities for Arabs, Indians, Africans, and Europeans.

In open-air village schools, the missionaries taught young Kenyans to read and write English and to work at trades, such as carpentry. They also attempted to eradicate native customs by teaching children to wear Western clothes, eat with utensils, and shun tribal rituals in favor of Christian traditions. For more than 50 years, the missionary system—the only educational program in Kenya—instructed natives in European ways.

Kenya's health services teach mothers about child care

75

When Kenya gained its independence in 1963, the government immediately created a public school system. The power of the mission schools declined as native Kenyans began attending integrated government schools, where they were taught in both Swahili and English and trained in a variety of fields. School attendance soared. By the late 1960s, more than 800,000 Kenyans were enrolled. Today—even though attendance is not mandatory—83 percent of Kenyan youngsters go to school.

Kenya has more than 8,000 primary schools, which the government funds either fully or in part. After seven years of primary (elementary) school, students who wish to further their education take a test known as the Kenya Preliminary Examination. If they pass, they can attend one of the more than 1,000 secondary schools funded by the government. At the end of four years, students take another examination to determine if they can enter college.

Although most Kenyans have traditionally chosen to further their education in England, enrollment is increasing at Kenya's colleges, universities, and technical schools. The ultra-modern University of Nairobi offers degrees in science, medicine, law, agriculture, engineering, architecture, education, and the arts. The Kenya Polytechnic Institute, also in Nairobi, meets the needs of industrial employers by offering training in a variety of industrial occupations. Kenya also has more than one dozen teacher training colleges that prepare students for careers in education.

Because Kenya's population is so young—almost 50 percent of Kenyans are under the age of 15—the need for qualified teachers and adequate educational facilities is enormous. The lack of teachers and adequate funding has recently forced schools to limit enrollments. The government has increased the Ministry of Education's budget so that it can afford to open more schools and train more teachers to meet the challenge of educating Kenya's young.

Health Care

Health care has improved dramatically in the past few decades. The number of medical professionals and hospital beds has risen, life expectancy has increased, and the infant mortality rate has declined. Today, Kenya has more than 1,600 doctors and 25,000 hospital beds. More than 150 health centers provide care for rural Kenyans, and the King George VI Hospital in Nairobi has an outpatient medical center for city-dwellers. Mission hospitals and other private medical facilities now exist in most Kenyan towns.

Several factors account for the dramatic improvement in health care. Since Kenya gained independence, the government has made an effort to eradicate superstitious practices and to provide modern health care to all its people. Kenyans have been educated in hygiene and preventive medicine, and the government has funded a number of health-care projects. Through the Flying Doctor program—in which health officials fly throughout the countryside teaching and caring for villagers—the government has brought sophisticated health care to rural areas.

The government had also provided funds for the diagnosis and control of infectious diseases. Medical research and increased public awareness have eliminated or greatly reduced many diseases. For example, sleeping sickness, a once-dreaded disease carried by

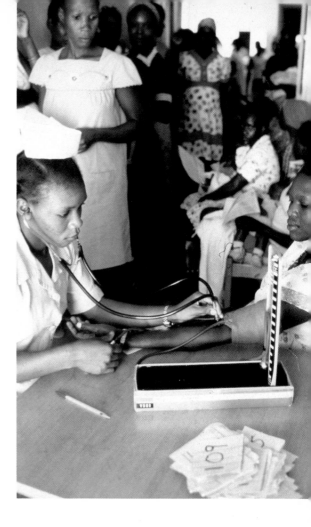

Women receive prenatal health care at a clinic in Kenya

the *tsetse* fly, can now be easily cured, and the *mwaba* fly, a dangerous insect whose bite causes blindness, has been exterminated. Health teams are working to decrease the incidence of malaria and hookworm and to wipe out bilharzia (schistosomiasis), a debilitating disease carried by parasites that burrow into the human skin and cause tissue damage, blood loss, and often, death.

Despite these advances, Kenya still lags behind the industrialized world in health care. In the United States, for example, life expectancy for a man is 71.6 years, whereas in Kenya it is only 56.3 years. But that figure represents a lifespan almost five years longer than that of less than a decade ago, proving that health care in Kenya is improving rapidly.

Transportation

As one of the most modern nations in East Africa, Kenya has a well-developed transportation system. Kenyans travel through their country

Kenya's transportation system includes modern highways and bridges

by car, boat, rail, and air. The Kenya-Uganda railway, completed in 1903, was the first step toward achieving swift travel in East Africa. Today, more than 4,000 miles (6,400 kilometers) of railway connect Kenya's towns and cities to the outside world. Rail lines now serve the agricultural highlands and the highly populated western regions.

A workman clears ground for a new highway across Kenya's expanse

For centuries, Kenya's ports and rivers have been vital trade routes. More than 2,800 miles (4,480 kilometers) of waterways are navigable by small boats, and modern seaports can service huge ships. Recently, cruise ships have begun to visit Mombasa from places such as the Seychelles, India, and various European and United States cities.

Kenya has two international airports and a number of smaller, local air fields. Nairobi International Airport has facilities for jumbo jets as well as small aircraft. Regular flights from Europe and the United States land at both Nairobi and Mombasa, Kenya's second international airport. Many villages now have small landing strips to accommodate health-care officials and others who participate in Kenya's Flying Doctor program.

Communications

Kenya's communications systems have greatly improved in recent decades. Today, Kenya has radio, television, newspapers, telephones, telex, and telegraph service. Radio broadcasts are the most common source of daily news in Kenya. The Kenya News Agency (KNA) and the Voice of Kenya (VOK) newsrooms have access to national and international information. Television—in both Swahili and English, the nation's two official languages—reaches about half the population.

The major English-language newspapers are the *Daily Nation*, the *Kenya Times*, and the *Standard*. The daily *Tafia Leo* is published in Swahili. A number of other newspapers are published in tribal languages, including *Liomon Le Maasai* for the Maasai people.

Touring Kenya

Since the late-19th century, tourism has played an important role in Kenya's economy. In the late 1800s, Europeans and Americans flocked to East Africa to hunt big game, such as elephants, rhinoceroses, and lions. But the government outlawed hunting long ago, and today visitors come to Kenya to enjoy the country's natural wonders. Miles of beaches, scores of mountains, and acres of parks attract thousands of visitors each year.

Elephants drink at a watering hole in one of Kenya's national parks

Chimpanzees and baboons live in the forests of Kenya

More than 6 million acres (2.4 million hectares) of Kenya's land have been set aside by the government for parks and game reserves. The largest, Tsavo National Park in southern Kenya, is home to lions, leopards, cheetahs, buffalo, rhinoceroses, and elephants. The Maasai Mara Game Reserve, 200 miles (320 kilometers) west of Nairobi, is the perfect vantage point from which to observe the wildebeests—large, ox-like creatures—that migrate through the countryside from June to November. Other parks include Sibiloi National Park, where many ancient ruins and Bronze Age artifacts have been found; Lake Victoria National Park, home to a variety of fabulous birds; and Aberdare National Park, where visitors can see and explore the vast Aberdare Mountains.

In Mount Kenya National Park near the town of Nyeri, visitors can explore Kenya's most magnificent mountain. Professional climbers can scale its glaciered peaks, and amateurs can negotiate lower elevations. More than half a dozen mountain lodges offer accommodations for tourists, and the Mountain Club of Kenya organizes climbing parties and provides information to mountaineers.

Adventurous visitors find Kenya the ideal spot for a safari. A typical safari includes two or three days on the plains, two days in the highlands, three days in the rugged, desert-like country around the mountains, and two days in western Kenya near Lake Victoria. Kenya is so popular with safari-goers that it has set up outposts in the most remote areas of the countryside to provide tourists with information, food, and lodging.

Those who would rather "rough it" can camp in any of Kenya's game reserves and national parks. Campers can buy or rent small huts called *bandas*, in which they can sleep and store their gear. Camping is perfectly safe, although one must be careful to avoid attracting animals. Baboons and elephants will charge a campsite if they smell fruits or vegetables, and bees will swarm if water is left unattended.

Kenya's coastal areas are popular for a number of reasons. White-sand beaches attract sunbathers, and coastal waters lure sailors and fishermen. During the official game-fishing season, from September to May, deep-sea fishermen can snare blue marlin, mako shark, and barracuda in the coastal waters. The government's Fisheries Department operates camps where novices can learn the fine points of deep-sea fishing.

Kenya also has a number of resorts where visitors can enjoy less adventurous entertainment, such as golf, tennis, and polo. It is one of the few places in the world where unspoiled nature lies only miles from modern, bustling cities.

Kenya's strength and unity promise a secure future for its youth

An Eye Toward the Future

Only 100 years ago, East Africa was a surviving example of life in the Stone Age. There were no roads, no established settlements, and no commerce or currency. People lived in small, isolated communities and practiced subsistence agriculture. Today, Kenya is the most modern country in all of black Africa. It has industrial manufacturing centers as well as posh vacation resorts.

This modernization has taken its toll on the country and its people. Rural tribespeople have seen their traditional lands swallowed up by encroaching cities, and the changing economy has left many farmers jobless. In some cases, attempts to help the rural poor have created new problems. For example, while the infant mortality rate has dropped dramatically, population growth has increased by more than 4 percent annually. This tremendous increase in population has caused a rise in unemployment, and thus, an increase in poverty and crime.

Despite these difficulties, Kenya remains the most prosperous country in East Africa. The famine that has plagued Ethiopia and its neighbors has not troubled Kenya. Its people are among the best-educated in East Africa, and the sons of tribal shepherds are today doctors, lawyers, and political leaders.

Kenyatta's achievements are a legacy for today's Kenyans

In the 1950s, Jomo Kenyatta wrote, "I hope peace and prosperity will come to our people, when all of us can unite and work for the purpose of uplifting our people, who have been struggling so hard for centuries." Kenya's government is working to fulfill this wish and to unite all of its people in a spirit of tolerance and understanding.

Index

ACKNOWLEDGMENTS AND PHOTO CREDITS

The author and publisher are grateful to these sources for information and photographs:
AP/Wide World Photos (pp. 32, 88); Kenya Tourist Office (pp. 37, 82); Library of
Congress (pp. 9, 14, 20, 22, 24, 26, 27, 29, 41, 44, 45, 48, 49, 51, 52, 55, 57, 58, 60, 64,
65, 67, 69, 73); National Museum of African Art/Smithsonian Institution (pp. 19, 83); H.
Armstrong Roberts, Inc. (front cover); World Bank Photo (pp. 2, 11, 12, 15, 18, 30, 35,
38, 39, 42, 46, 54, 56, 59, 62, 70, 71, 74, 75, 78, 79, 80, 86). Picture research:
Imagefinders, Inc.

93